DATE DUE			

TOP 10 FOOTBALL QUARTERBACKS

William W. Lace

SPORTS TOP 10

ENSLOW PUBLISHERS, INC.

44 Fadem Road	P.O. Box 38
Box 699	Aldershot
Springfield, N.J. 07081	Hants GU12 6BP
U.S.A.	U.K.

Library of Congress Cataloging-in-Publication Data

Lace, William W.
    Top 10 football quarterbacks / William W. Lace.
        p. cm.—(Sports top 10)
    Includes bibliographical references (p.) and index.
    ISBN 0-89490-518-X
    1. Football players—United States—Biography—Juvenile literature.
2. Quarterback (Football)—Juvenile literature. [1. Football players.] I. Title.
II. Title: Top 10 football quarterbacks. III. Series.
GV939.A1L33 1994
796.332'092'2—dc20
[B]   93-40469
                                              CIP
                                               AC

Printed in the United States of America

10 9 8 7 6 5 4

Illustration Credits: The Indianapolis Colts, pp. 43, 45; Cleveland Browns, p. 19; Cleveland Plain Dealer, Cleveland, Ohio, p. 21; Dallas Cowboys Weekly, pp. 38, 41; Denver Broncos Photo, pp. 15, 17; Photo courtesy of Houston Oilers, pp. 30, 33; Photo courtesy of the Miami Dolphins, pp. 23, 25; © Michael Zagaris, pp. 26, 29; Pittsburgh Steelers/Michael F. Fabus, pp. 10, 13; From the collections of the Texas Sports Hall of Fame, pp. 6, 9; Vernon Biever, pp. 35, 37.

Cover Illustration: Denver Broncos Photo.

Interior Design: Richard Stalzer.

CONTENTS

INTRODUCTION — 4

SAMMY BAUGH — 6

TERRY BRADSHAW — 10

JOHN ELWAY — 14

OTTO GRAHAM — 18

DAN MARINO — 22

JOE MONTANA — 26

WARREN MOON — 30

BART STARR — 34

ROGER STAUBACH — 38

JOHNNY UNITAS — 42

NOTES BY CHAPTER — 46

INDEX — 48

INTRODUCTION

WHAT DOES A PERSON NEED to be a top quarterback in the National Football League? Let's make a list.

First, he must be a good passer. Pro football now depends more and more on the passing game. So the first requirement for a quarterback is that he has to be able to throw. He must be able to look down the field for receivers while tacklers are coming after him.

The quarterback must be able to run, too. When all receivers are covered, when there is no place to throw, the quarterback must be able to scramble. Sometimes he must dodge tacklers until he finds a receiver. Other times, he must run the ball himself. Then he takes the same kinds of hits as his running backs. (Running backs are also called halfbacks or fullbacks.)

The quarterback must be like a magician. He must be able to take the snap from the center, put the ball in a running back's stomach, pull it out at the last minute, and hide it behind one leg.

The quarterback must be able to think, too. He must be able to come to the line of scrimmage, "read" the defense, and then adjust the play. He must know where everyone on the offense is supposed to be on every play. He tells them where to line up if they forget.

The quarterback must be able to gamble. When everyone thinks he should pass, he has to be ready to call a running play. When everyone expects a run, he should be ready to throw. Sometimes, if he needs four yards for a first down, he should be willing to go for forty and a touchdown.

The quarterback must be the leader, the general, the boss

of the offense. He may listen to advice, but he has the final word. There is no time in the huddle for a vote, no time for arguments.

It is also almost impossible to pick ten men and say that they are the top ten quarterbacks in the history of professional football. There are probably forty quarterbacks who would make someone's top ten list. But, a "Top Ten" list can contain only ten names. So here is *my* list.

CAREER STATISTICS

Player	Seasons	Attempts	Completions	Percent	Yards	Interceptions	Touchdowns
SAMMY BAUGH	16	2,995	1,693	56.5	21,886	203	188
TERRY BRADSHAW	14	3,901	2,025	51.9	27,989	210	212
JOHN ELWAY	15	6,894	3,913	56.8	48,669	216	278
OTTO GRAHAM	6*	1,565	872	55.7	13,499	94	88
DAN MARINO	15	7,452	4,453	59.8	55,416	220	385
JOE MONTANA	15	5,391	3,409	63.2	40,551	139	273
WARREN MOON	14*	6,528	3,827	58.6	47,465	224	279
BART STARR	16	3,149	1,808	57.4	24,718	138	152
ROGER STAUBACH	11	2,958	1,685	57.0	22,700	109	153
JOHNNY UNITAS	18	5,186	2,830	54.6	40,239	253	290

*National Football League only.

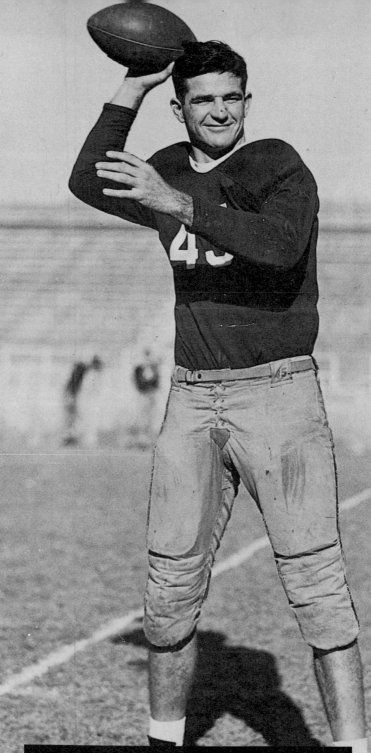

SAMMY BAUGH

Sammy Baugh revolutionized professional football by becoming the first quarterback to use a passing attack.

SAMMY BAUGH

BEFORE SAMMY BAUGH APPEARED, PLAYERS used the pass mostly when a team was behind, distance was long, and time was short. It was Baugh who "made the forward pass a routine play from scrimmage."[1]

The Chicago Bears found that out the hard way. It was early in the 1937 NFL championship game. The Washington Redskins lined up in punt formation on their own nine-yard line. Baugh, a skinny rookie from Texas, was deep in the end zone.

Instead of kicking, he shocked the Bears with a short pass to Cliff Battles. Battles went all the way to midfield. The Bears were stunned! In those days, quarterbacks almost never passed from deep in their own territory. They *never, ever* passed from their own end zone. Baugh went on to hit 17 of 34 passes for 358 yards that day. That included three touchdown passes in a twelve-minute time span.

Baugh was a star football player in Sweetwater, Texas. He improved his accuracy by throwing balls through an old tire that was swinging from a tree branch. He started playing as an end. When he threw the ball back to the quarterbacks much faster than they threw it to him, the coaches switched him. He played college football at Texas Christian University. There coach Dutch Meyer taught him to fake and scramble until a receiver broke open.

Baugh actually got his nickname—"Slingin' Sam"— when he played baseball. In fact, he wanted to play professional baseball much more than he did football. He wound up signing to play both—baseball with the St. Louis Cardinals and football for the Washington Redskins. Fortunately for football, his baseball career lasted only one year.

During his sixteen year NFL career, he was a great passer. He led the league six times. Baugh was also perhaps the best punter in history. He set records for a season average (51.4 yards) and a career average (45.1 yards). But that's not all. He was a talented defensive back. In all, he made 28 career interceptions.

But Baugh is best remembered for being an accurate passer. Soon after he joined the Redskins, coach Ray Flaherty diagrammed a play on the blackboard. "When he [the receiver] gets here, Sam," Flaherty said, "I want you to hit him in the eye with the ball." Baugh replied, "Which eye?"[2]

His backup quarterback, Harry Gilmer, said, "He could throw overhanded, sidearmed, even underhanded, and all at different speeds, never setting his feet the same way twice."[3]

He was one of the first quarterbacks to develop a "quick release," where he quickly cocked his arm and threw the ball. In those days, linemen could hit the quarterback after he threw the ball until the play was whistled dead. Baugh had to get rid of the ball fast and then duck!

He was a complete player and a fierce competitor. When Redskins owner George Marshall told him to quit going downfield to make tackles after punts, Baugh quit punting altogether. "There is no point in playing if you can't try to do your absolute best to be the best you can," he said.[4]

Baugh changed football almost single-handedly. After he began using the pass to lead the Redskins to championships, other teams developed passing attacks. The game became more exciting, and fans grew more interested.

When the Pro Football Hall of Fame opened in 1963, Baugh was named a charter member. In 1987, members of the Pro Football Researchers Association voted informally to select the best football player ever. The easy winner was Sammy Baugh.

SAMMY BAUGH

BORN: March 17, 1914, Temple, Texas.

HIGH SCHOOL: Sweetwater High School, Sweetwater, Texas.

COLLEGE: Texas Christian University.

PRO: Washington Redskins, 1937–1952.

RECORDS: NFL Career Punting Record, 45.1 yard average.

HONORS: Pro Football Hall of Fame, 1963.

Baugh goes over the top quarterbacking for the Washington Redskins in a game with the New York Giants, December 9, 1937. The Redskins had just moved from Boston, where they were known as the Braves.

TERRY BRADSHAW

Terry Bradshaw was known for his famous throwing arm as well as his strong character.

"HE COULDN'T SPELL CAT IF you spotted him the 'C' and the 'A,' " the Dallas Cowboys' Thomas Henderson said about Terry Bradshaw. That was before the Cowboys and Bradshaw's Pittsburgh Steelers met in Super Bowl XIII.[1]

Nobody ever questioned how good Bradshaw's arm was. It was his head they were worried about. People called him dumb.

After that game, however, it was Henderson who looked dumb. Bradshaw threw for 318 yards and four touchdowns, and he was named the Most Valuable Player. "I was labeled a winner," he said. "Sports isn't about IQ. It's about winning and losing."[2]

During the game, Bradshaw showed his poise and confidence in the face of a furious Cowboy comeback. He didn't always have that confidence, though.

He had always had the arm. When he was a boy in Shreveport, Louisiana, he would throw a football fifty to one hundred times every day. If he didn't have a friend to play catch with, he'd throw into a bucket or through a tire.

When he was a high school senior, he passed for 1,400 yards and 21 touchdowns. He showed just how powerful his right arm was by throwing the javelin 243 feet. This set a national high school record.

Still, he questioned his own ability. Instead of going to Louisiana State, which had a big-time football program, he went to Louisiana Tech. This was a much smaller college and it was closer to Shreveport. By the time he finished playing there, the pro scouts said he'd be the number one pick in the 1970 draft.

Sure enough, he was. The Steelers won the right to choose first by flipping a coin with the Chicago Bears. When Bradshaw signed his contract with the Steelers, his father predicted that his son would lead Pittsburgh to the Super Bowl.

During his first years with the team, Bradshaw didn't lead anyone anywhere. He hit only 4 of 16 passes in his first game. In his rookie year, he threw three interceptions in a game. He was booed by the fans. Sportswriters began to say that he wasn't smart enough for pro football.

"There were a lot of problems," he said. "I had a lot of growing up to do."[3]

The growing up came in 1974. Bradshaw was a part-time starter until mid-season. Then, things started to click. The Steelers went on to win their first Super Bowl. Bradshaw's father's prediction came true. There were three more Super Bowl victories in the 1970s. Bradshaw was voted Most Valuable Player in the last two.

Bradshaw is not one of the NFL's best quarterbacks in yardage, touchdown passes, or accuracy. His best physical asset was his strong arm, but plenty of quarterbacks had strong arms. Even Bradshaw himself said, "I doubt that I'll ever be able to look in the mirror and say, 'I'm the best quarterback in professional football.' "[4]

His statistics were good. In fact, he led the American Football Conference in passing in 1978. But, what set Bradshaw apart was his strength of character. Like Otto Graham of the Cleveland Browns, he was a winner. He was the first quarterback to win four Super Bowls.

The Pittsburgh Steelers teams of the 1970s were full of stars. There were Franco Harris, Lynn Swann, John Stallworth, and Mean Joe Greene. But they had only one leader, Terry Bradshaw. Greene had it right when he said during the 1974 season, "The Bradshaw the whole world thinks it knew, that's all over."[5]

TERRY BRADSHAW

BORN: September 12, 1948, Shreveport, Louisiana.

HIGH SCHOOL: Woodlawn High School, Shreveport, Louisiana.

COLLEGE: Louisiana Tech University.

PRO: Pittsburgh Steelers, 1970–1983.

HONORS: Most Valuable Player, Super Bowls XIII, XIV.
Pro Football Hall of Fame, 1989.

Terry Bradshaw was the first quarterback to win four Super Bowl rings. Joe Montana tied his record in 1990.

JOHN ELWAY

THE DENVER BRONCOS' HOPES OF making Super Bowl XXI were fading. They had the ball on their own two-yard line. The Cleveland Browns led, 20–13, with only five minutes thirty-two seconds to go.

In the huddle, receiver Steve Watson looked at his quarterback, John Elway. "He smiled," Watson recalled, "I couldn't believe it. And he said, 'If you work hard, good things are going to happen.' "[1]

They did. Elway scrambled out of trouble and hit his receivers. Denver moved to the Cleveland five. Then, with thirty-nine seconds left to play, Elway hit Mark Jackson in the end zone. The extra point tied the game, and the Broncos went on to win in overtime. In Denver, it became known simply as "The Drive."

Elway did work hard, but he also had natural athletic ability. Sports were very important to the Elway family. His father was a coach. Once, the family interrupted a vacation to drive young John fifty miles to Little League practice.

When he was fifteen years old, Elway decided to concentrate on football. He broke records at Granada Hills High School in Los Angeles, California. He went on to break records at Stanford University.

Elway was considered the best pro prospect in the country in 1983. The Baltimore Colts made him the first person taken in that year's draft. Elway did not want to play for Baltimore, he said, because he did not want to play for superstrict coach Frank Kush. He said he might play baseball instead. Finally, Baltimore traded the rights to Elway to the Denver Broncos.

JOHN ELWAY

Out of the shotgun, John Elway scrambles downfield. Elway's overall athletic ability and strong will to win have made him one of the top quarterbacks in the league.

John was a starter during his rookie year. He had a rough time, though, and coach Dan Reeves benched him. He came back strong toward the end of the season, however, and Denver made the playoffs.

Elway continued to improve. After "The Drive" in 1986, he led Denver to the Super Bowl again the next season. One reason for his success was that the Broncos sometimes used the "shotgun" formation to take advantage of Elway's passing ability.

The Broncos went to Super Bowl XXIV, too. Unfortunately for Elway, they lost. In fact, he has been the losing quarterback in three Super Bowls. "I think personally, he'll be better from it and more determined than ever," said Reeves.[2]

Elway's greatness comes from a combination of overall athletic ability, a strong passing arm, and a very strong will to win. "He's got the mobility of Fran Tarkenton and the arm of Joe Namath," said former Philadelphia Eagles coach Buddy Ryan.[3] In 1987, in fact, John was the second-leading rusher for Denver.

"Elway doesn't have quite the numbers," said former Los Angeles Raiders coach Mike Shanahan, "but he's still the best in the game. He can carry a team on his own phenomenal athletic ability and his intense desire to win."[4]

Time after time, Elway rallied the Broncos from what seemed sure defeat. There was "The Drive" in 1986. And, in the 1991 playoffs, John directed an 87-yard drive with just 2 minutes 7 seconds remaining and no timeouts. The Broncos beat the Houston Oilers, 26–24.

In the 1997 season, Elway finally won the big one. Behind his inspiring leadership the Broncos reached Super Bowl XXXII, defeating the Green Bay Packers, 31–24.

"In the years to come, John will be the *best* that ever was," said former teammate Gerald Wilhite, "if he isn't already."[5]

JOHN ELWAY

BORN: June 28, 1960, Port Angeles, Washington.

HIGH SCHOOL: Granada Hills High School, Los Angeles, California.

COLLEGE: Stanford University.

PRO: Denver Broncos, 1983– .

RECORDS: NCAA, Most touchdowns in a single game, 6; NCAA, First quarterback to throw more than 2,500 yards in three straight years.

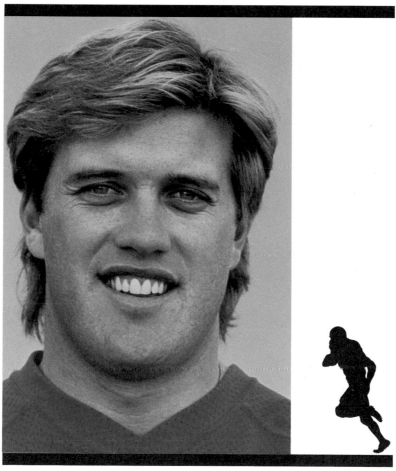

The first player chosen in the 1983 NFL draft, Elway has led the Denver Broncos to four AFC championships, including one Super Bowl victory.

OTTO GRAHAM

IN FIVE MINUTES, OTTO GRAHAM turned from bad guy into hero. He couldn't have picked a better day. It was the 1950 NFL championship game between Graham's Cleveland Browns and the Los Angeles Rams.

Late in the fourth quarter Graham brought the Browns to within one point. But, when the Browns got the ball back, Graham fumbled. The game seemed lost.

Fortunately, the Browns' defense held again and Graham got another chance. He fooled the Rams by running the ball himself on the first play. That gained 19 yards. Then he hit on three passes to work the ball to the Los Angeles eleven-yard line. Only a few seconds were left in the game. From there, Lou Groza kicked the winning field goal. Graham had led the Browns to a 30–28 win and the NFL championship in the team's first year in the league. Not bad for a man who didn't play college football until his junior year!

He went to Northwestern University on an athletic scholarship, but it was for basketball. Growing up in Waukegan, Illinois, Graham's favorite sport was basketball. He practiced by tossing tennis balls into a wastebasket in his room.

Graham played intramural football for fun at Northwestern. He was such a star that the coaches convinced him to go out for the varsity team. By the time he was a senior, he was named the Most Valuable Player in the Big Ten Conference.

When Graham graduated from college in 1943, the country was in the middle of World War II. He served in the Navy for two years, but he continued to play football.

In 1945, Paul Brown was coach of the Cleveland Browns in the new All America Football Conference. He remembered

Otto Graham was one of the NFL's most accurate passers. He led his team to ten title games in his ten years as a Cleveland Brown.

OTTO GRAHAM

seeing Graham play in college. He particularly liked one play on which Graham ran to his left, then threw back to his right to score a touchdown. "I asked myself, 'What kind of player is this?' " Brown recalled, "and he was the first man I picked for my Cleveland team."[1]

Graham and the Browns won four championships and had a record of fifty-two wins, four losses, and two ties in the next four years. This success contributed to the end of the All America Football Conference. Cleveland simply had no competition. The Browns joined the NFL in 1950.

Some people thought the Browns couldn't compete in the older league. The team promptly showed that it could. Graham threw three touchdown passes in the season opener. They beat the defending champion Philadelphia Eagles. Cleveland went on to beat the Los Angeles Rams for the championship. Graham called this victory "the biggest thrill of my career."[2]

Graham's strongest point as a quarterback was his accuracy. In the 1950 championship game, for instance, he was 22 for 32—almost 70 percent! He completed 55.7 percent of his passes over a 10-year career. This "defined greatness for pro quarterbacks."[3] His specialty was the sideline pass. Receivers would run downfield, then cut for the sideline. Graham would hit them—time after time—just before they stepped out of bounds.

"Otto had amazing coordination between hand and eye," said Browns receiver Dante Lavelli. "He could react in a split second when he saw his receiver, and at the same moment, he was anticipating not only the receiver, but what the defensive man would do."[4]

Above all, Otto Graham was a winner. In his ten years in professional football, Cleveland played in ten straight title games. They won seven. "The test of a quarterback is where his team finishes," his coach, Paul Brown, said. "So by that standard, Otto was the best of them all."[5]

Otto Graham

BORN: December 6, 1921, Waukegan, Illinois.

HIGH SCHOOL: Waukegan High School, Waukegan, Illinois.

COLLEGE: Northwestern University.

PRO: Cleveland Browns, 1946–1955.

HONORS: Pro Football Hall of Fame, 1965.

Otto Graham was an all-around athlete. He had the strength and speed needed to run with the ball, as well as the skill to throw accurate passes.

DAN MARINO

THE GAME WAS IN MIAMI, but Dan Marino had to be thinking "Pittsburgh." First, the Dolphins were playing the Pittsburgh Steelers for the 1984 AFC Championship. The winner would play in Super Bowl XIX. Second, Pittsburgh was Marino's home town. He had been a star in both high school and college there. He had also cheered Steelers quarterback Terry Bradshaw.

But Marino, who was the Dolphins' quarterback, was now all business. The Steelers led early. Shortly before halftime, Marino took control of the game. He hit pass after pass. Miami scored on five straight possessions and overwhelmed Pittsburgh, 45–28. Marino had destroyed his hometown team by passing for 421 yards and 4 touchdowns.

When Marino was a boy, playing sports was a family affair. Dan's father worked nights. He was always home after school to play catch or hit grounders. His dad was the one who taught Marino the one thing that has set him apart from all the other quarterbacks—a quick release.

He taught his son to bring the ball back to his ear and flick it with his wrist. Today, Marino can take the ball from the center and get a pass off as quickly as 1.5 seconds. This is much faster than most other quarterbacks. For this reason, he doesn't get sacked as often. "He doesn't bring the ball up and throw it with that long arm motion," said Don Shula, his coach. "It's 'boom' and the ball's gone with a tremendous whip of the shoulders."[1]

Dan played college football at the University of Pittsburgh. As a junior, he threw 37 touchdowns. Everyone thought he would win the Heisman Trophy when he was a

DAN MARINO

Dan Marino drops back to pass. Marino uses a quick release style of throwing the ball which keeps him from getting sacked.

senior. His senior season, however, was so-so. He was the twenty-seventh player taken in the 1983 pro draft. "Sure, my pride was stung," he said, "but I never, for a moment, started doubting what I could do on a football field."[2]

It was a great bargain for the Dolphins. Marino was the starter by the sixth game of his rookie year. He led the NFL in passing. He became the first rookie ever to be a starter in the Pro Bowl.

This was good, but it was nothing compared to Marino's 1984 season. He hit an amazing 64.2 percent of his passes. He set an NFL record of 5,084 yards. His 48 touchdown passes were also an NFL record. In 1991, he became only the fourth player in NFL history to pass for more than 35,000 yards. And he did it in just nine seasons.

Most experts agree that Marino has the best arm in pro football. But, he also has the heart and the head to go with it. "No matter what's thrown against him," writer John Holstrom said, "he'll stand in there and take it, and do what he has to to get his team moving."[3]

He's also a fierce competitor, and he is the unquestioned leader of the Miami offense. He doesn't hesitate to correct his teammates if he feels they're doing something wrong. "He'll jump on your stuff right in the huddle," said Dolphin receiver Mark Duper.[4]

No doubt about it. Marino is confident, almost cocky. He says what is on his mind. He told a reporter while he was still at Pittsburgh, "I throw better than anyone in college. And I can throw with anyone in the pros. There, that's what I think."[5]

Marino, however, has backed up his talk with action. No less an expert than former Pittsburgh Steeler quarterback Terry Bradshaw said, "Dan Marino's the best quarterback I've ever seen."[6]

DAN MARINO

BORN: September 15, 1961, Pittsburgh, Pennsylvania.
HIGH SCHOOL: Central Catholic High School, Pittsburgh,
           Pennsylvania.
COLLEGE: University of Pittsburgh.
PRO: Miami Dolphins, 1983– .
RECORDS: NFL, Most yards in a season, 5,084; Most touchdown
    passes (Career), 385; Most yards passing (Career), 55,416.

Marino holds the record for the most passing yards in a season, 5,084.
Although he has yet to win the Super Bowl, he has made the Miami
Dolphins into a winning team.

JOE MONTANA

Looking for his man, Montana drops back to pass. Along with his exceptional throwing abilities, Joe Montana uses his instincts to beat his opponents.

JOE MONTANA

IN NFL HISTORY, IT'S KNOWN as "The Catch." But, for every catch, there's a throw. This one was by Joe Montana.

Only fifty-eight seconds were left in the NFC championship game in 1981. Montana and the San Francisco 49ers trailed the Dallas Cowboys, 27–21. They had the ball, third-and-goal at the Dallas six-yard line.

Montana took the snap and came under a heavy rush. He saw receiver Dwight Clark cutting across the end zone. Montana was off-balance and falling backwards, but he threw the ball high. "It would likely guarantee that if D. C. didn't catch the ball no one else would," he wrote later.[1]

Montana didn't see the end of the play. He didn't have to. The roar of the San Francisco fans told him all he needed to know. It was a touchdown and the 49ers' ticket to Super Bowl XVI.

Montana had bought crucial time on the play with a pump fake. This got Cowboy Ed "Too Tall" Jones to jump too soon. "Hey," Montana wrote, "it was just like basketball with Dad. A fake would usually get him up in the air when we went one-on-one in the playground."[2]

Joe Montana, Sr., was often tired when he came home from work in Monongahela, Pennsylvania. But he was never too tired to play with Joe, Jr. He was always there—shooting baskets, going out for passes, catching his son's fastballs.

Once, Montana wanted to quit football. His father said, "If you want to quit, you can. But only after you finish playing out the year. I don't want you ever to quit anything you've already started."[3] Young Joe stuck with sports.

Montana's favorite sport was basketball. But, he realized

that if he wanted to be a pro athlete, it would have to be as a football player. He chose to attend the most famous football school of all—Notre Dame. When he was a junior, he led the Fighting Irish to the Cotton Bowl. There they upset top-ranked Texas. In the next year's Cotton Bowl, he brought Notre Dame back from a score of 34–12 to beat Houston, 35–34. This was when he earned the nickname "Comeback Kid."

He was not considered a particularly outstanding pro prospect. San Francisco took him in the third round of the 1978 draft. He rode the bench most of his first two seasons. That changed in 1980. The 49ers were 6-10, but Joe convinced Bill Walsh, his coach, that he could be the number one quarterback.

He did become his team's top quarterback. And he also turned into one of the game's all-time bests. He has consistently been among the top-rated passers in the NFL. He's been a leader in all the statistical categories—yardage, touchdowns, percentage of passes completed. He and Pittsburgh's Terry Bradshaw are the only quarterbacks to win four Super Bowls.

He has a very good arm, but it is not the greatest one ever. Instead, he uses his mind; he out-thinks the opposing defense. "For a quarterback," he wrote, "the game is at least 70 percent mental."[4] He also relies on gut feelings. Bill Walsh said that Montana "is the most instinctive quarterback ever to play the game."[5]

However, his most outstanding quality is based on his father's advice. He never gives up. Time after time, the "Comeback Kid" brought his team back from what seemed to be certain defeat. "When the game is on the line," said Walsh, "and you need someone to go in there and win it right now, I would rather have Joe Montana than anybody else who ever played the game."[6]

JOE MONTANA

BORN: June 11, 1956, Monongahela, Pennsylvania.

HIGH SCHOOL: Ringgold High School, Monongahela, Pennsylvania.

COLLEGE: University of Notre Dame.

PRO: San Francisco 49ers, 1979–1992; Kansas City Chiefs, 1993–1994.

RECORDS: NFL, Most Consecutive Passes Completed, 22.

HONORS: Most Valuable Player, Super Bowls XVI, XIX, XXIV.

Montana is one of only two quarterbacks to win four Super Bowl rings. Trying for a fifth, Montana brought the Kansas City Chiefs all the way to the AFC championship game in his first year on the team.

WARREN MOON

Moon looks for an open man downfield. Although he has not enjoyed the spotlight as much as other quarterbacks, Moon is the master of the run-and-shoot offense.

WARREN MOON

THEY DIDN'T STOP THE GAME. There was no celebration. Warren Moon hurried his Houston Oilers back into the huddle. Nobody noticed that history had just been made.

It was only a seven-yard pass from Moon to Drew Hill. Houston was trying to catch the New York Giants on a cold, windy day in New York. The next day's *Houston Post* did not mention that Moon was now the first NFL quarterback to complete 400 passes in one season.

The week before he had broken Dan Marino's record of 378. Nobody seemed to notice that either. That's the story of Moon's career—breaking records and not getting much attention.

Moon grew up in Los Angeles, California. He was a high school All-American, but he didn't get much attention from college scouts. He spent his freshman year at a junior college. After a year, he won a scholarship to the University of Washington.

When he was a senior at Washington, Moon was Pac-10 Conference Player of the Year and Most Valuable Player in the Rose Bowl. He still didn't get much attention. NFL scouts said he'd go no higher than the fourth round of the draft. So he signed with Edmonton of the Canadian Football League.

His combination of passing and running made him a superstar in Canada. In that country, quarterbacks run more often than in the NFL. He led Edmonton to five straight championships.

This finally got him some attention. He signed a contract with the Oilers in 1984. Then he had a string of good, but not great, seasons. That changed in 1990 when new coach Jack Pardee brought the "run-and-shoot" offense to the Oilers.

In the run-and-shoot, the quarterback takes a short drop or rolls out, either throwing to one of four wide receivers or running himself. "If ever a player was born for a system, that player is Moon," Paul Zimmerman wrote.[1]

In one 1990 game, he threw for 527 yards against the Kansas City Chiefs. Former NFL coach Sid Gilman said, "I've never seen a better exhibition of throwing the football than in his performance . . . and I've seen a lot of football games."[2] He might have broken Marino's record that year, but he dislocated a thumb in the next-to-last game of the season.

He broke the record in 1991. In 1992 he was bothered by injuries, so he passed for only 2,521 yards. Even so, he was the American Football Conference's top-rated passer.

Moon's combination of passing and running ability make him one of the most dangerous men in football. He's good at any type of pass. Houston offensive coordinator Kevin Gilbride called his pass "a gorgeously tight spiral, probably the prettiest pass in the National Football League."[3]

He also is one of the best at throwing on the move—a must in the run-and-shoot offense. He's a tough runner. He'll dive headfirst for extra yards. He has a great vision of the playing field. He's mentally quick enough to keep track of his four wide receivers and the four pass routes each one of them might run on any play.

Moon was thirty-seven years old at the end of the 1993 season. He probably won't have a chance at the all-time passing yardage record. One wonders what he would have accomplished if the six years he spent in Canada had been spent in the NFL. He might have received the attention he deserves.

"Somehow, I never seem to be spoken of in the same breath with the really top names in the game," he said. "Well, hopefully, there's still time."[4]

WARREN MOON

BORN: November 18, 1956, Los Angeles, California.

HIGH SCHOOL: Hamilton High School, Los Angeles, California.

COLLEGE: University of Washington.

PRO: Edmonton Eskimos, 1978–1983; Houston Oilers, 1984–1993;
    Minnesota Vikings, 1994–1996; Seattle Seahawks, 1997– .

RECORDS: NFL, Most Passes Completed, Season (1991), 404.

HONORS: Most Valuable Player, Rose Bowl, 1978.

Moon is one of the highest rated passers in the AFC and has
helped the Houston Oilers become a winning team for the first time
since 1980.

BART STARR

BART STARR PASSED FOR MORE than 24,000 yards during his 16-year football career. He later said, though, that "the most significant play of my life," was a one-yard run.[1] Starr's Green Bay Packers trailed the Dallas Cowboys, 17–14, in the 1967 NFL championship game. Only sixteen seconds remained in the game. The Packers had the ball at the Cowboy one-yard line.

The temperature was below zero. Lambeau Field in Green Bay, Wisconsin, was frozen solid. Starr thought he could keep his footing on a quarterback sneak, though.

The play was the "31 wedge." Starr took the snap from center Ken Bowman, followed the block of right guard Jerry Kramer, and squeezed into the end zone. The Packers were now the NFL champs. They went on to defeat the Kansas City Chiefs, 35–21, in Super Bowl I.

Starr was at his best in the big games. In his six NFL championship games, he completed 69 percent of his passes for 11 touchdowns. Only two of the attempted 145 passes in those games were intercepted. He was Most Valuable Player in both Super Bowls I and II. He was elected to the Pro Football Hall of Fame in 1977.

It was a remarkable record for a man who almost quit football when he was in the tenth grade. Bart was discouraged when he didn't make the varsity high school team in Montgomery, Alabama. He told his father he was quitting. His father said that was fine. Bart would now have time to work cleaning up the garden. The next day, Bart was the first person on the practice field.

Starr became an all-state quarterback. Then he played at

In his sixteen seasons as a Green Bay Packer, Bart Starr led the NFL in passing three times and set the NFL record for the most consecutive passes without being intercepted.

the University of Alabama. He was a starting player as a sophomore. But he missed his junior year because of an injury. A new coach put him on the bench most of his senior year. Alabama basketball coach Johnny Dee brought him to the attention of the Packers. They drafted him in the seventeenth round in 1956.

He was a backup for more than three seasons. Coaches didn't have confidence in him. Finally, Packer coach Vince Lombardi made him the starter late in 1959. The Packers won their last four games. They reached the championship game the next year. They were NFL champs five of the next seven years. Starr led the league in passing in 1962, 1964, and 1966. In 1966, he was named NFL Player of the Year.

Starr didn't have the athletic ability of some other top quarterbacks. He relied instead on what writer Mickey Herskowitz called "his own deep and deceptive stock of raw nerve."[2] He was gentlemanly and soft-spoken off the field, but he was a tough competitor on it. "A quarterback has got to be as tough as a guard," said former teammate Jim Colvin. "Starr is that way."[3]

Starr was one of the smartest, coolest quarterbacks ever. "Nothing seems to rattle him" said Detroit Lions linebacker Joe Schmidt. "You can never get him mad, and that's what we like to do, get the quarterback all excited and mad."[4]

He had a knack for knowing what the other team was expecting, then he did something else. "You can't take any kind of a gamble against him," said San Francisco 49ers coach Dick Voris. "A gamble produces a weakness and he always finds it."[5]

BART STARR

BORN: January 9, 1934, Montgomery, Alabama.

HIGH SCHOOL: Sidney Lanier High School, Montgomery, Alabama.

COLLEGE: University of Alabama.

PRO: Green Bay Packers, 1956–1971.

HONORS: Most Valuable Player, Super Bowls I, II;
Pro Football Hall of Fame, 1977.

Bart Starr was the winner of the Most Valuable Player award in the first two Super Bowls ever played.

ROGER STAUBACH

Known as "Roger the Dodger" because of his scrambling ability, Roger Staubach won all of football's highest honors, including the Heisman Trophy in college and the Super Bowl MVP award.

ROGER STAUBACH WANTED A TOUCHDOWN so badly that it almost ended his career. It wasn't a Super Bowl. It was just a preseason game between Staubach's Dallas Cowboys and the Los Angeles Rams.

Staubach went back to pass, but he couldn't find a receiver. So he ducked under a defensive lineman and took off down the left sideline. When linebacker Marlin McKeever came up to meet him, Staubach ducked his head and drove straight into him.

"I didn't want to go out of bounds," he wrote later. "I wanted to score."[1]

Instead, he severely separated his right shoulder. That play caused Staubach to miss most of the 1972 season. But it was typical of his all-out style of play. His style made him one of the NFL's great quarterbacks.

Staubach was like that as far back as Purcell High School in Cincinnati, Ohio. There his scrambling earned him the nickname "Roger the Dodger." He rushed for more than 500 yards his senior year, even though his team didn't have a single play that called for the quarterback to run.

Even early in his pro career, Staubach was not like other scrambling quarterbacks. He refused to slide to the ground when defenders closed in. "Fran Tarkenton [the Minnesota Viking quarterback] lies down before you can hit him," said Buddy Ryan, then an assistant with the New York Jets. "This guy Staubach thinks he's a running back."[2]

Staubach and his parents lived in Silverton, near Cincinnati. He had no brothers and sisters, but there were plenty of kids in the neighborhood. Roger started playing team sports when he was six.

He was a devout Roman Catholic. He wanted to play football at Notre Dame, a Catholic college, after high school. Forty colleges recruited him, but Notre Dame was not one of them. So, he went to the U.S. Naval Academy. In his junior year, he led Navy to a 9-2 season. That same year he won the Heisman Trophy as the top college player in the country.

Staubach was drafted in 1965 by both the Dallas Cowboys and the Kansas City Chiefs. The Chiefs were in the American Football League then. He chose the Cowboys. He still had four years to serve in the Navy after graduation. After serving two years in Vietnam, he spent the last two years playing football at the Pensacola, Florida, Naval Air Station. He came to the Cowboys training camp in 1969. He was a twenty-seven year-old rookie, but coach Tom Landry had confidence in him.

Staubach was Dallas' number-two quarterback. Craig Morton was first. Staubach became the starter midway through the 1971 season. He led the Cowboys to their first Super Bowl title over the Miami Dolphins. Roger Staubach was named Most Valuable Player in that game.

He missed most of the 1972 season, but he led the Cowboys to the NFC championship game in 1973. Staubach guided Dallas to four NFC titles and two Super Bowl victories before he retired in 1980. He led the NFL in passing four times, and he was named to six Pro Bowls.

When Staubach retired, he was the all-time leader in passing efficiency, and he also had run for 2,264 yards. His tremendous desire to win, however, set him apart. Twenty-three times he brought the Cowboys from behind in the fourth quarter to win. Often it was in the game's final seconds.

Tom Landry summed it up best: "Roger Staubach might be the best combination of a passer, an athlete, and a leader ever to play in the NFL."[3]

ROGER STAUBACH

BORN: February 5, 1942, Silverton, Ohio.

HIGH SCHOOL: Purcell High School, Cincinnati, Ohio.

COLLEGE: U.S. Naval Academy.

PRO: Dallas Cowboys, 1969–1979.

HONORS: Most Valuable Player, Super Bowl VI;
Pro Football Hall of Fame, 1985.

Although Dallas lost two of its four Super Bowl appearences, Roger Staubach is tied with Joe Montana and Terry Bradshaw for quarterbacking in four Super Bowls.

JOHNNY UNITAS

MANY SAY IT WAS THE GREATEST game ever. It was the 1958 NFL championship game. The Baltimore Colts trailed the New York Giants, 17–14. Two minutes were left. The Colts had the ball on their own fourteen-yard line. Johnny Unitas was quarterback.

Unitas passed to Lenny Moore for a first down at the twenty-five. Then he hit Raymond Berry, his favorite receiver, for 25, 15, and 22 yards. There were seven seconds left. A field goal sent the game into sudden death.

The game was now in overtime. Unitas moved his team from its own twenty to the Giants' eight. Everybody thought the Colts would run the ball, then kick a field goal. Unitas fooled them all. He threw a sideline pass to Jim Mutscheller. Mutscheller went out of bounds at the one. Alan Ameche scored on the next play, and the Colts were champions. One writer called his performance "a textbook example of how to direct a team under pressure."[1]

It had taken hard work to get where Unitas was now. He was born in Pittsburgh, Pennsylvania. When his father died, his mother kept the family coal-delivery business going. The young Johnny grew strong shovelling coal. He was paid seventy-five cents a ton.

Unitas played college football at the University of Louisville. There he set fifteen school records, but Louisville had losing seasons his last three years. The Pittsburgh Steelers picked him in the ninth round of the 1955 draft. He was later cut. He wound up playing semipro ball for the Bloomfield Rams. His salary was six dollars a game! His real job was as a construction worker.

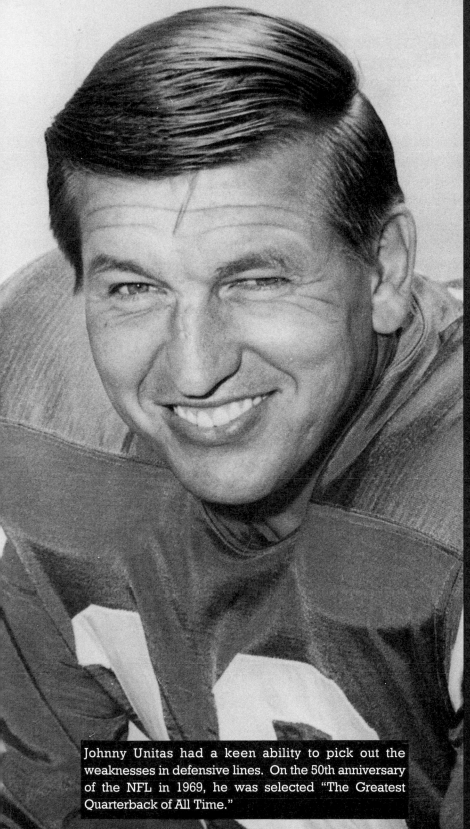

JOHNNY UNITAS

Johnny Unitas had a keen ability to pick out the weaknesses in defensive lines. On the 50th anniversary of the NFL in 1969, he was selected "The Greatest Quarterback of All Time."

He got another chance in the pros in 1956. He made the Baltimore Colts as the number-two quarterback. When starter George Shaw was injured, Unitas took over. He led the Colts to three championships. He was voted the NFL's Most Valuable Player three times. In 1979, he entered the Pro Football Hall of Fame.

He held most NFL passing records when he retired. The most amazing one is still not broken. From 1956 to 1960, Unitas threw at least one touchdown pass in 47 straight games.

Unitas had all the physical tools. He had a quick setup and delivery, and he had an arm like a cannon. He was deadly on short passes, and he specialized in the long bomb. "He lets fly with the intention of putting the ball right in the man's hands," said Coach Weeb Ewbank. "It's no accident when he does it. He means to do it, believe me."[2]

He was physically tough and a fierce competitor. Once his nose was broken by a defensive lineman. He stuffed mud up his nostrils to stop the bleeding and kept on playing. On the field he was the boss. "Nobody talks in the huddle except me," he once wrote. "At that point, suggestions can only cause trouble."[3]

He was a thinker as well as a thrower. He could spot weaknesses in a defense and pick it apart. "You can't fool Unitas," said cornerback Willie Brown. "Unitas knows. No matter what you do, Unitas knows."[4]

He wasn't afraid to gamble. "You've got to have the guts of a burglar," a coach once said, "and this guy Unitas may be the biggest burglar of them all."[5]

Baltimore beat the Giants again for the championship in 1959. New York linebacker Sam Huff summed it up. "Unitas is great," he said. "No one around even compares with him."[6]

Johnny Unitas

Born: May 7, 1933, Pittsburgh, Pennsylvania.

High School: St. Justin's High School, Pittsburgh, Pennsylvania.

College: University of Louisville.

Pro: Baltimore Colts, 1956–1972; San Diego Chargers, 1973.

Honors: Pro Football Hall of Fame, 1979.

Unitas led the Baltimore Colts to an amazing five NFL championships and two Super Bowls. When Unitas retired in 1973, he held most NFL passing records.

NOTES BY CHAPTER

Sammy Baugh
1. Mickey Herskowitz, *The Quarterbacks* (New York: William Morrow and Company, 1990), p. 24.
2. Arthur Daley, *Pro Football's Hall of Fame* (New York: Grosset and Dunlap, 1963), p. 163.
3. George Sullivan, *The Gamemakers: Pro Football's Greatest Quarterbacks—From Baugh to Namath* (New York: G. P. Putnam's Sons, 1971), p. 9.
4. Beau Riffenburgh and David Boss, *Great Ones: NFL Quarterbacks From Baugh to Montana* (New York: Penguin Books, 1989), p. 30.

Terry Bradshaw
1. Don Pierson, *Terry Bradshaw* (Chicago: Childrens Press, 1981), p. 39.
2. Mickey Herskowitz, *The Quarterbacks* (New York: William Morrow and Company, 1990), p. 285.
3. Terry Bradshaw, *Looking Deep* (Chicago: Contemporary Books, 1989), p. 195.
4. Pierson, p. 41.
5. "Terry Bradshaw," *Lincoln Library of Sports Champions,* vol. 3 (Columbus, Ohio: Frontier Press Company, 1989), p. 7.

John Elway
1. "John Elway," *Lincoln Library of Sports Champions,* vol. 4 (Columbus, Ohio: Frontier Press Company, 1989), p. 68.
2. Larry Fox, *Sports Great John Elway* (Hillside, New Jersey: Enslow Publishers, 1990), p. 61.
3. Rick Telander, "Tough Guy in the Clutch," *Sports Illustrated* (January 26, 1987), p. 32.
4. Beau Riffenburgh and David Boss, *Great Ones: NFL Quarterbacks From Baugh to Montana* (New York: Penguin Books, 1989), p. 70.
5. Ralph Wiley, "Getting Better and Better," *Sports Illustrated* (November 10, 1986), p. 70.

Otto Graham
1. Mickey Herskowitz, *The Quarterbacks* (New York: William Morrow and Company, 1990), p. 242.
2. George Sullivan, *The Gamemakers: Pro Football's Greatest Quarterbacks—From Baugh to Namath* (New York: G. P. Putnam's Sons, 1971), p. 46.
3. Herskowitz, p. 242.
4. George Sullivan, *Pro Football's All-Time Greats* (New York: G. P. Putnam's Sons, 1968), p. 138.
5. Sullivan, *The Gamemakers*, p. 49.

Dan Marino
1. Lou Sahadi, *The Official 1986 Miami Dolphins Guidebook* (Dallas: Taylor Publishing Company, 1986), p. 25.
2. Dan Marino, *Marino!* (Chicago: Contemporary Books, 1986), p. 51.
3. John Holmstrom, *Dan Marino/Joe Montana* (New York: Avon Superstars, 1985), p. 56.
4. Ibid., p. 4.

5. Ibid., p. 12.

6. Bob Rubin, *Dan Marino: Wonder Boy Quarterback* (Chicago: Childrens Press, 1985), p. 10.

Joe Montana

1. Joe Montana and Bob Raissman, *Audibles* (New York: William Morrow and Company, 1982), p. 82.

2. Ibid., p. 81.

3. Ibid., p. 91.

4. "Joe Montana," *Lincoln Library of Sports Champions*, vol. 10 (Columbus, Ohio: Frontier Press Company, 1989), p. 53.

5. Mickey Herskowitz, *The Quarterbacks* (New York: William Morrow and Company, 1990), p. 311.

6. Beau Riffenburgh and Dave Boss, *Great Ones: NFL Quarterbacks From Baugh to Montana* (New York: Penguin Books, 1989), p. 53.

Warren Moon

1. Paul Zimmerman, "The Big Moon Launch," *Sports Illustrated* (November 5, 1990), p. 69.

2. "Houston Oiler Media Guide," 1992, p. 101.

3. Robert Draper, "Blue Moon," *Texas Monthly* (December, 1992), p. 154.

4. Zimmerman, p. 70.

Bart Starr

1. Bart Starr, *My Life in Pro Football* (New York: William Morrow and Company, 1987), p. 6.

2. Mickey Herskowitz, *The Quarterbacks* (New York: William Morrow and Company, 1990), p. 254.

3. Edwin Shrake, "A Rumor is Scotched and a Starr Revived," *Sports Illustrated* (October 30, 1967), p. 24.

4. Starr, p. 141.

5. "Bart Starr," *Lincoln Library of Sports Champions*, vol. 15 (Columbus, Ohio: Frontier Press Company, 1989), p. 50.

Roger Staubach

1. Roger Staubach, *First Down, Lifetime to Go* (Waco, Texas: World Books, 1974), p. 250.

2. George Sullivan, *Roger Staubach: A Special Kind of Quarterback* (New York: G. P. Putnam's Sons, 1974), p. 113.

3. Beau Riffenburgh and Dave Boss, *Great Ones: NFL Quarterbacks From Baugh to Montana* (New York: Penguin Books, 1989), p. 47.

Johnny Unitas

1. Beau Riffenburgh and Dave Boss, *Great Ones: NFL Quarterbacks From Baugh to Montana*, (New York: Penguin Books, 1989), p. 39.

2. Johnny Unitas and Ed Fitzgerald, *Pro Quarterback: My Own Story* (New York: Simon and Schuster, 1965), p. 48.

3. Ibid., p. 96.

4. Ibid., p. 125.

5. George Sullivan, *The Gamemakers: Pro Football's Great Quarterbacks—From Baugh to Namath* (New York: G. P. Putnam's Sons, 1971), p. 125.

6. Ibid., p. 126.

INDEX

A
Ameche, Alan, 42

B
Battles, Cliff, 7
Baugh, Sammy, *6–9*
Berry, Raymond, 42
Bowman, Ken, 34
Bradshaw, Terry, *10*–13, 22,
    24, 28, 41
Brown, Paul, 18, 20
Brown, Willie, 44

C
Clark, Dwight, 27
Colvin, Jim, 36

D
Duper, Mark, 24

E
Elway, John, 14–17
Ewbank, Weeb, 44

F
Flaherty, Ray, 8

G
Gilbride, Kevin, 32
Gilman, Sid, 32
Gilmer, Harry, 8
Graham, Otto, 12, 18–21
Greene, Joe "Mean Joe," 12
Groza, Lou, 18

H
Harris, Franco, 12
Henderson, Thomas, 11
Hill, Drew, 31
Huff, Sam, 44

J
Jackson, Mark, 14
Jones, Ed "Too Tall," 27

K
Kramer, Jerry, 34
Kush, Frank, 14

L
Landry, Tom, 40
Lavelli, Dante, 20
Lombardi, Vince, 36

M
Marino, Dan, 22–25
Marshall, George, 8
McKeever, Marlin, 39
Meyer, Dutch, 7
Montana, Joe, 13, *26*–29, 41
Moon, Warren, *30*–33
Moore, Lenny, 42
Morton, Craig, 40
Mutsheller, Jim, 42

P
Pardee, Jack, 32

R
Reeves, Dan, 16
Ryan, Buddy, 16, 39

S
Schmidt, Joe, 36
Shanahan, Mike, 16
Shaw, George, 44
Shula, Don, 22
Stallworth, John, 12
Starr, Bart, 34–37
Staubach, Roger, *38*–41
Swann, Lynn, 12

T
Tarkenton, Fran, 16, 39

U
Unitas, Johnny, 42–45

V
Voris, Dick, 36

W
Walsh, Bill, 28
Watson, Steve, 14
Wilhite, Gerald, 16